Oscar Wilde's Stories on Stage
A collection of plays based on
Oscar Wilde's stories

Oscar Wilde's Stories on Stage

First published in 2017
by
JemBooks
Cork,
Ireland
dramastartbooks.com

ISBN: 978-0-9935506-3-8

Oscar Wilde's Stories on Stage
A collection of plays based on Oscar Wilde's stories

Julie Meighan

JemBooks

About the Author

Julie Meighan is a lecturer in Drama in Education at the Cork Institute of Technology. She has taught Drama to all age groups and levels. She is the author of the Amazon bestselling *Drama Start: Drama Activities, Plays and Monologues for Young Children (Ages 3 -8)* ISBN 978-0956896605, *Drama Start Two: Drama Activities and Plays for Children (Ages 9-12)* ISBN 978-0-9568966-1-2 and *Stage Start: 20 Plays for Children (Ages 3-12)* ISBN 978-0956896629.

Contents

Oscar Wilde's Stories on Stage

Oscar Wilde (1854-1900)

The plays in this collection are adapted from Oscar Wilde's short stories. Oscar Wilde was a popular novelist and a playwright who lived in late Victorian times.

Chronology of Oscar Wilde's Life

1854: Wilde was born in Dublin. His mother was, Lady Jane Francesca Wilde (1820-1896) a successful poet and journalist. His father, Sir William Wilde (1815 - 1876) was a renowned eye surgeon.

1864 – 1871: He attended Portora Royal School, Enniskillen.

1871 – 1874: He attended Trinity College, Dublin where he received a royal scholarship to read Classics.

1874-1879: He attended Magdalen College, Oxford. He read the Greats, which was the name given to an undergraduate course which focused on Classics (Ancient Rome, Ancient Greece, Latin, ancient Greek and philosophy.) He graduated with a double first.

1878: Wilde wins the Newdigate Prize for *Ravenna* (poem).

1881: His first collection of poetry – *Poems* were published - the book received some critical praise and established Wilde as an up-and-coming writer.

1882: He wrote his first play – *Vera or the Nihilists*. The play was not successful.

1883: He wrote his second unsuccessful play, *The Duchess of Padua*.

1884: Wilde married Constance Lloyd (1859-1898).

1885: Their son, Cyril, was born (1885-1915). He was killed by a German sniper during WW1.

1886: Their youngest son, Vyvyan, was born (1886-1967).

1888: *The Happy Prince and Other Tales*, his children's stories was published.

1891: Wilde published two collections of short stories - *Lord Arthur Savile's Crime and other Stories*, and *A House of Pomegranates*. *The Picture of Dorian Gray* is also published, his first and only novel. It was first published in *Lippincott's Magazine*, 1890, and then published in book form, revised and expanded by six chapters in 1891.

1892: He wrote two successful plays: *Lady Windermere's Fan* and *Salome*.

1893: He wrote *A Woman of No Importance*.

1894: He wrote *The Importance of Being Earnest*. This along with *The Picture of Dorian Gray* are considered to be amongst the great literary masterpieces of the Victorian era.

1895: He wrote *An Ideal Husband*. At the height of his theatrical success, he is arrested for homosexual offenses. He is found guilty for the crime of sodomy and sentenced to two years of hard labor.

1898: He wrote his best known poem, *The Ballad of Reading Gaol*. His wife, Constance, died.

1900: Oscar Wilde died of cerebral meningitis in Paris. He was 46 years old.

Wilde's Witticisms

Oscar Wilde is known for his witty sayings. Here are my top 20 Oscar Wilde quotes.

The world is a stage, but the play is badly cast.

Always forgive your enemies; nothing annoys them so much.

The only thing to do with good advice is pass it on. It is never any use to oneself.

What is a cynic? A man who knows the price of everything and the value of nothing.

Anyone who lives within their means suffers from a lack of imagination.

All women become like their mothers. That is their tragedy. No man does. That's his.

Genius is born—not paid.

Morality is simply the attitude we adopt towards people whom we personally dislike.

The old believe everything, the middle-aged suspect everything, the young know everything.

There is only one thing in life worse than being talked about, and that is not being talked about.

Be yourself; everyone else is already taken.

To live is the rarest thing in the world. Most people exist, that is all.

If you want to tell people the truth, make them laugh, otherwise they'll kill you.

A man's face is his autobiography. A woman's face is her work of fiction.

I don't want to go to heaven. None of my friends are there.

A thing is not necessarily true because a man dies for it.

You don't love someone for their looks, or their clothes, or for their fancy car, but because they sing a song only you can hear.

Never love anyone who treats you like you're ordinary.

It takes great deal of courage to see the world in all its tainted glory, and still to love it.

Live! Live the wonderful life that is in you! Let nothing be lost upon you. Be always searching for new sensations. Be afraid of nothing.

The Happy Prince

Characters: Grandad, two grandchildren, three town councillors, Mother, Little Boy, Swallow, five swallows, Young Writer, Teacher, two schoolchildren, Match Girl, Melter

Child 1: We are bored. Granddad, wake up.

Child 2: Wake up, Granddad. We are bored; we have played with all our toys and we have nothing else to do.

Child 1: Granddad, will you tell us one of your stories?

Granddad: Of course I will. Children, come over here and sit down. Have I told you the story of the Happy Prince?

Children: No.

Granddad: Well, long, long time ago, high above the city, there stood the most beautiful statue. It was the statue of the Happy Prince.

Child 1: What did he look like?

Granddad: He was covered all over with fine gold. He had two bright sapphires for his eyes and a large red ruby glowed on the top of his sword. *(Statue is standing centre stage, very still.)*

Town Councillor: *(Looks up at the statue with admiration.)* He is as beautiful as a weathercock. Unfortunately he is not very useful during these hard times. *(Mother and Little Boy enter; Little Boy is crying.)*

Mother: Why are you crying?

Little boy: Because I want to go to the moon.

Mother: Why can't you be like the Happy Prince? He never dreams of crying for anything.

Town Councillor: I'm glad there is someone in this city that is happy.

(They walk off.)

(Enter some school children and their teacher.)

School child 1: *(Looks up at the statue.)* He looks like an angel.

Teacher: How do you know what an angel looks like?

School child 2: We have seen them in our dreams.

Teacher: Don't be ridiculous. Everybody knows children don't dream.

(Six swallows come flying in and land near the statue.)

5

Swallow 1: It is getting cold now.

Swallow 2: We should go to warmer climes.

Swallow 3: I was thinking of Florida.

Swallow 4: We can't go to Florida, as there are lots of hurricanes there.

Swallow 5: I have a good idea. Let's go to Egypt.

Swallow: I can't go. *(Looks like he is in love.)*

Swallow 1: Why ever not?

Swallow 2: You will freeze if you stay here.

Swallow: You know, I have fallen in love with the most beautiful reed I have ever seen.

Swallow 3: Oh how romantic. Please tell us how you met. I love romantic stories.

Swallow: Well, I was chasing a yellow moth down by the river and there she was…

(Re-enacts the scene.)

Swallow: Oh my! You are the most beautiful reed I have ever seen.

Reed: Why thank you, Mr. Swallow.

Swallow: I shall love you forever.

Reed: Why, of course!

Grandad: The reed made him a low bow so he flew around her, touching the water with his wings and making silver ripples. This romance lasted through the summer.

Swallow 4: This is ridiculous.

Swallow 5: She has no money and too many cousins.

Swallow 3: I think it is romantic.

Swallow 1: Well we are off. Are you coming or not?

Swallow 2: Ask her to come with you because you can't stay here.

(Swallow flies to the river and sees the reed.)

Swallow: Reed, will you come to Egypt with me?

Reed: Of course not. My home is here with my cousins.

Swallow: You have been playing with my feelings. I'm off to find my friends and we are going to the pyramids.

(Swallow flies off.)

Grandad: By the time he reached the city, it was night and his friends had gone. He took shelter on the feet of the Happy Prince statue. As he was just about to fall asleep, a drop of water fell on him.

Swallow: How strange. There is not a single cloud in the sky, the stars are clear and bright and yet it is raining.

(Another drop falls.)

Swallow: What a useless statue; it can't keep the rain off. It is not rain, it is the statue. He is crying. Why are you crying, Happy Prince?

Happy Prince: When I was alive and had a human heart, I played all day in the palace and I never cared what happened outside the palace. I lived such a happy life, but now I'm dead and I'm up here. I can see all the misery and hardship in my city.

Swallow: What can I do to help?

Happy Prince: Take the ruby from my sword and give it to the woman whose son has a fever and who can't afford oranges.

Woman: What can I do to make it better?

Little Boy: I want some oranges.

Woman: We can't afford them.

(Swallow drops off the ruby and the woman finds it.)

Woman: Maybe we can afford oranges after all.

(Swallow returns to the Happy Prince.)

Swallow: I must go to Egypt to be with my friends.

Happy Prince: Just stay one more day and be my messenger. I see a young man in a small room. He is trying to finish a play for the director of the theatre, but he is too cold to write. He has fainted from hunger. Pluck out one of my eyes and give it to him so he can sell it to the jeweller and buy food and firewood and finish his play.

Swallow: I can't do that.

Happy Prince: Do as I command you.

(The swallow drops the sapphire off in the young man's room.)

Young writer: I am beginning to be appreciated; this must be from a great admirer.

(Swallow has returned to the statue.)

Swallow: I've come to say goodbye.

Happy Prince: Swallow, Swallow, will you not stay one more night? I need your help. In the square is a little Match Girl. She has dropped her matches and her father will beat her. Pluck out my other eye and give it to her.

(Swallow drops the sapphire in front of the Match Girl.)

Match Girl: Oh what a beautiful stone. *(She runs home laughing.)*

Swallow: You are blind now so I will stay with you always.

Happy Prince: No, little Swallow. You must got to Egypt to be with your friends in the warm climate.

Swallow: I will stay with you always. *(Falls asleep at the prince's feet.)*

Happy Prince: I'm covered with fine gold. You must take it off, leaf by leaf, and give it to the poor.

Granddad: The swallow did just that—leaf after leaf of fine gold he gave to the poor. The children's faces grew rosier and rosier and they laughed and played games. The winter came and the swallow grew colder and colder, but he would not leave the prince. He knew he was going to die.

Swallow: Goodbye, dear Prince. Will you let me kiss your hand?

Happy Prince: I'm glad you are going to Egypt at last. You must kiss me on the lips for I love you.

Swallow: I am not going to Egypt but to the house of death.

(Swallow kisses the prince and falls down dead at his feet.)

Granddad: Just then there was an almighty crack from inside the statue. His lead heart had snapped in two.

Town Councillor: The statue looks very shabby, and look at this dead bird at his feet. *(Points to the dead swallow.)* We must issue a law that birds are no longer allowed to die. We need to take down the statue. He is no longer beautiful.

Granddad: They then melted the statue down.

Melter: What a strange thing—this broken heart will not melt in the furnace. I will throw it away.

(He throws it into the rubbish bin next to where the dead bird was laying.)

The Selfish Giant

Characters: The Selfish Giant; The Cornish Ogre; 3 parts of the wall: Sad, Lazy and Frightened; 2 Trees; Ice; Frost; Snow; Wind; Narrator/Old man; 8 Children: Anna/Billy/Cathy/Ger/Dick/Ellie/Fred/Harry; 2 grandchildren.

(Curtains are closed. The opening scene is an old man sitting with his two grandchildren grouped around him, sitting downstage left. Selfish Giant and Cornish Ogre are sitting centre stage, miming drinking tea and talking.)

Narrator/Old man: Children come over here and I will tell you the story of a giant that lived a long time ago. He had a lovely, beautiful garden with soft, green grass. There were the most amazing flowers and twelve fabulous peach trees. However, the giant was very selfish, and he shared his garden with no one.

Old Man: He used to say...

Selfish Giant: My own garden is my own garden and no one else can use it!

Old Man: The giant had been to visit his friend the Cornish Ogre and stayed seven years.

(Giant and Ogre drink tea and mime having a conversation.)

Selfish Giant: I have been here for seven years, and we have run out of things to talk about.

Cornish Ogre: Yes, you have been here a long time, so maybe it is time you went back to your beautiful, empty garden.

Old Man: They said goodbye and the Selfish Giant returned home.

(Giant waves goodbye and they both leave the stage, going in different directions.)

Old Man: However, what the Selfish Giant didn't know was that his garden was being used by the local school children.

(School bell rings. Eight children run up the centre aisle and start to play with the children in the audience. They run down the side aisles and reach the steps to the stage. The curtains open and there is a wall, centre stage, with three parts to it. There is the happy part of the wall; a frightened part of the wall; and a lazy part of the wall. The lazy part is in the centre. There are also two trees on

each side of the stage: centre stage left and centre stage right. The children squeeze through a hole in the wall.)

Anna: Right, I've got through! Come on, Cathy. I'll give you a hand. Mind the nettles.

Billy: Ouch! Take care, Cathy, the nettles are very bad today. Watch out.

Cathy: All right. Nearly through. *(She pushes her way in.)* That's it. Here at last. *(Sighing.)* Wonderful!

(Children chat as four more go through the hole, one-by-one.)

Dick: *(The last one is trying to get through but has difficulty.)* This hole seems to be getting smaller and smaller, unless it's my imagination.

Ellie: No, you've got that wrong, Dick. You're getting fatter. It's all that fast food you eat.

(Children all laugh and pull Dick through the hole.)

Ger: I love this place so much, and I am so happy when we are all in here playing.

(Everyone agrees by nodding their heads.)

Harry: It's been seven years since the giant was here. I know it's his garden, but he can't come back after all this time, can he?

Fred: I hope not. But just in case, we'd better make the most of it while we've got it.

(Children go off-stage. Lights focus on the three parts of the wall.)

Frightened: Wake up, Lazy. If the Selfish Giant comes back, we will be in trouble.

Lazy: The giant hasn't been here for seven years. I am tired of holding up the centre of the wall.

Happy: I love seeing all the children playing in the garden. I am so happy when they come into the garden, but, Lazy, I think you should wake-up.

Lazy: I am going back to sleep. *(Starts snoring.)*

Frightened: I'm scared. I have a bad feeling.

Happy: You are always scared. Try to cheer up and be happy that the sun is shining and the children are having such a good time playing in the garden.

Tree 1: Lazy needs to wake up.

Tree 2: Why don't we ask the audience to help us?

Tree 1: That's a good idea. When we count to three, everyone must say, "Wake-up, Lazy."

Happy, Frightened and the trees: One, two, three audience, everybody together: Wake-up, Lazy.

(Eight Children come back on the stage and the trees and the two parts of the wall freeze.)

Fred: Let's play a game of Stuck in the Mud!

Ger: No, that's really boring.

Ellie: I know! Let's play Giant's Footsteps.

Billy: That's not funny.

Dick: What about Blind Man's Bluff?

All: Oh yes!

Cathy: Here's my tie. Come on, Fred. Ready for the blindfold?

Fred: I'm not doing it.

Anna: You are a scaredy-cat.

All except Fred and Harry: Scaredy-cat; scaredy-cat.

Harry: Leave him alone, I will do it.

(Harry is blindfolded and the game begins. They run around having fun. There is the sound of footsteps.)

Tree 1: Did you hear that?

Tree 2: Hear what?

Frightened: I heard it too. Wake up, Lazy.

Lazy: I'm sleeping.

(Giant enters while the children are playing.)

Happy: Lazy, I think you need to wake up. NOW!

(All the children see the giant and they begin to squirm and then all run away.)

Giant: How on earth did those horrible children get inside my garden?

(Looks at the wall and sees Lazy only half-standing up.)

Giant: I see where the problem is. Lazy, wake up now!

(Lazy jumps up and stands at attention.)

Frightened: *(Whispers.)* I told you he was going to come back.

Giant: Wall, if you don't stand up properly, I am going to knock you down and build a new, stronger wall. This is my garden and NO ONE is allowed in here. I know what I'm going to do. I'm going to put up a sign.

(Giant gets a sign and puts it around Lazy's neck.)

Giant: *(Shouts at the children.)* Can you read this sign, you horrible children?

Children: Trespassers will be persecuted.

11

Giant: No, you ignorant children. It is TRESPASSERS will be PROSECUTED.

Lazy: What does that mean?

Happy: It means anyone will be in trouble if they come into the garden.

(Giant exits, muttering. Curtains close to change the scene.)

Narrator/Old Man: Now the children had nowhere to play.

(Curtains open. The stage has changed, as the trees are now behind the wall and they are all upstage to give the illusion that the children are outside the garden.)

Anna: Why does the giant have to be so mean?

Billy: We have nowhere to play now.

Cathy: We weren't doing him any harm.

Dick: Where will we play now?

Ellie: The road!

Fred: We could get knocked down.

Ger: We have no choice now.

(The children look forlorn and play with their heads down. They all look toward the garden.)

Harry: How happy we were there!

(The children slowly walk off the stage.)

Narrator/Old Man: Spring came over the country. There were flowers blooming, trees in blossom and birds singing. Only in the garden of the selfish giant it was still winter. The birds did not care to sing in it as there were no children. And the flowers had no heart to bloom.

Ice: Well, Frost, I think our work has been done here.

Frost: I'm looking forward to having a break.

(Ice suddenly notices the sign: "Trespassers will be prosecuted.")

Ice: Look at this.

Frost: That Selfish Giant won't share his garden.

Ice: I know. Let's stay here until the Selfish Giant learns to share his beautiful garden.

Frost: I know, I will call Wind and Snow and get them to come and help. *(Takes out a mobile phone and rings them. Wind shows up immediately.)*

Wind: What's the big emergency? I was very busy in Florida. It is hurricane season, you know.

Ice: Wait until Snow gets here and we will tell you all about it.

(A few seconds later, Snow arrives on stage.)

Snow: I'm here.

Wind: What took you so long?

Snow: I was in Lapland helping Santa. What's the big emergency?

Frost: Anyway, look at this sign. The Selfish Giant won't share his garden, so we are going to stay here until he changes his mind.

(Ice, Frost, Wind and Snow freeze. Giant enters stage left, looking sad.)

Narrator/Old Man: The giant was very sad. A year passed and he began to realise he was very selfish. One day he saw one of the children under a tree crying and he went to help him.

(Giant mimes seeing the child. Nobody else can see him.)

Giant: Please, let me help. *(He reaches under the tree and mimes lifting up a child.)* I have been a very selfish giant. I will open my garden up to everyone. *(He takes down the sign and exits.)*

Ice: Frost, I think he has learned his lesson.

Frost: It's time to go. I heard there is an ogre in Cornwall who hasn't been very nice.

Ice: Wind and Snow, come on. It is time to go.

Snow: Do you have a map?

Frost: No! But I have my new Sat Nav/GPS.

Ice: Come on, let's go!

(They leave the stage. One of the children spies a hole in the wall and climbs through. He calls the others.)

Fred: I can't believe we are inside the garden again!

Dick: It's spring time.

Billy: Winter has gone.

Cathy: And there's no notice. The giant's notice is gone!

Harry: And the garden is more beautiful than ever.

(The children hear the giant's footsteps and hide behind the trees. Giant comes on stage and sees them. He waves them over. They are frightened but they move towards him slowly.)

Giant: Now I would like to join your games, if you please! *(Suddenly looking around.)* But where is your little friend?

Anna: What are you talking about, sir?

Billy: Do you mean Fred over there?

Fred: He doesn't mean me. He means Dick. *(He pushes Dick forward.)*

Dick: Did you want something *(stuttering nervously)*, Mmmmister…ssssir…Mmmister … Fffffriendly…Giant?

Giant: I want to know where the little boy is, the one that I lifted up into the branches of the tree.

Ellie: But we haven't been in the garden since you put the sign up. Well not until today.

Fred: Then we heard your footsteps.

Anna: So we hid by the wall. I'm sorry that we trespassed in your garden, Mr. Giant.

(All apologize, suddenly worried that the giant might become selfish again.)

Giant: Oh no, no, no. You don't need to say sorry. I am the one who is sorry. Please think of this garden as yours now. But I wish you could tell me where the little child lives. I am very fond of him because it is through him that I realised I had been selfish with my garden. No wonder spring never came!

Ger: But this is all of us. No one else came with us.

Billy: But we will ask around in school tomorrow and see if we can find out about your little friend.

Giant: Oh, yes, please. Now I really must have my rest. My old bones ache from all the playing. You carry on playing.

(Giant sits on the side of the stage and the children continue to play in slow motion.)

Narrator/Old Man: The years passed but the children were never able to find out who the giant's little friend had been. The giant grew very, very old. He could no longer play, so he sat in a huge armchair and watched the children. They all feared he would die soon.

(Giant mimes seeing the small child and calls out to him. Only Giant can see the small child. The children all stop playing immediately when they hear Giant talking. They look around but they can't see anyone.)

Giant: There he is! Come on, little friend. Where have you been? I've waited so long for you. Come and join in the fun. *(He hobbles towards the child.)* My goodness, how I've missed you! I had a feeling I might die before you came to see me again. *(Giant moves to hug the child, and then draws back in horror as he takes the child's hands and examines them.)*

Giant: Why, who has dared wound you? Tell me quickly, and I'll fetch my sword and kill him.

Small Child: *(Audience just hears the voice, they don't see small child; the voice can be done by the teacher or drama facilitator.)* No, these are the wounds of love.

Giant: *(Suddenly in awe.)* Who are you?

Small Child: Once you let me play in your garden. Today, you shall come with me to a very special garden called Paradise.

(Giant sinks slowly to the ground. The small child kneels beside the giant, makes him comfortable and comforts him. The children, aware Giant has died, sadly gather flowers and places them around him.)

The Canterville Ghost

Characters: Lord Canterville, Mr Otis, Mrs Otis, Virginia, James, Lewis, Clark, (Lewis and Clark are twins), Mrs Umney and Sir Simon (the ghost).

(Outside Canterville Castle there is a sign for sale which Lord Canterville is taking down.)

Scene 1: Canterville Castle

Lord Canterville: Well, it looks like we have a deal, Mr Otis. The castle is yours.

Mr Otis: Thank you, Lord Canterville. I'm sure my family will be very happy here. *(They shake hands.)*

Lord Canterville: *(Looks at him hesitantly.)* Perhaps, I should mention that Canterville Castle is haunted by a ghost. *(Ghost walks in behind them. They don't see the ghost but the audience does.)*

Mr. Otis: I don't believe in ghosts, Lord Canterville, so I'm sure I have nothing to be frightened of. *(They exit the stage.)*

(Mr and Mrs Otis and their four children, Virginia, James, Lewis and Clark, enter. They are greeted by an old woman dressed in an apron.)

Mrs Umney: Welcome, I'm Mrs Umney the housekeeper. Please, come in. There is tea in the library. *(There is a table and two chairs on the left side of the stage. Mr and Mrs Otis sit on them and Mrs Umney serves them tea.)*

Virginia: It is so exciting.

James: I know, let's explore. *(The four children run around the stage. They mime opening and closing doors.)*

Lewis: Look what's that? *(He picks a note up from the floor.)*

Clark: It's a note.

Virginia: Let me see.

James: If a child enters the secret room and stays until dead of night.

Lewis: Then at last Sir Simon can sleep in his tomb and at Canterville all will be alright.

Clark: What does that mean?

(Meanwhile in the library Mrs Otis is inspecting the ground carefully.)

Mrs Otis: I'm terribly sorry, Mrs Umney. I think I spilled something on your carpet.

Mrs Umney: That's not tea, it is blood.

Mr Otis: We must get rid of it. *(The children all come in and inspect the blood stain on the carpet.)*

Mrs Umney: I'm afraid that is impossible. That is the blood of Lady Eleanor Canterville. She was murdered by her husband Sir Simon Canterville 500 years ago. Then, Sir Simon disappeared and his body has never been found. They say his spirit haunts the house.

Lewis: I'll get rid of it. *(He rubs it.)*

Clark: Look it's gone.

(Then there is thunder and lightning and Mrs Umney faints. Lights go out. When the lights come back on, the blood stain is back.)

Mr Otis: Maybe the house is haunted after all.

Scene 2: Night in the Castle

(Mr and Mrs Otis are asleep in bed. There is a strange ratting noise and it was getting louder and louder. Mr Otis gets up and puts on his slippers and dressing gown. He opens the door and there in front is the ghost in chains.)

Mr Otis: Oh, you must be Sir Simon.

Sir Simon: *(Nods.)* Yes I am. *(He rattles his chains really loudly.)*

Mr. Otis: Here, take this bottle of oil *(he hands the bottle to the ghost)* and oil your chains. They are making too much noise. I can't sleep. *(Sir Simon throws the bottle on the ground and runs away and starts to make haunting noise.)*

(The two twins come on stage rubbing their eyes.)

Lewis: What's going on?

Clark: Who is making all that noise? *(They stop and share at the ghost.)*

Lewis: It's the ghost.

Clark: Here, throw your pillow at him to scare him *(They throw the pillows and run off stage.)*

Sir Simon: Well, I never. I have been scaring people for nearly 500 years and I have never been treated like this. Don't worry, I will get my revenge.

Scene 3: The Next Morning.

(Family are sitting at the table for breakfast.)

Mrs Otis: Children, you mustn't be frightened of the ghost.

Mr. Otis: Well, he didn't look very scary to me. (*Sir Simon comes out from the other side of the stage and stares at the family.*)

Sir Simon: I will exact my revenge on those pesky children.

(*The following is all done through mime. The children dress up as ghosts and scare Sir Simon. They hold a piece of string and trip him up. They put oil on the floor and he slips. They run off laughing. This can be done with music in the background.*)

Sir Simon: I'll stop those children once and for all. I'll appear as my most terrifying characters Reckless Rupert. Reckless Rupert always scares people. (*He tiptoes into the children's room and a bucket of water is thrown on him. The children laugh and he goes off dejected.*)

Lewis: We haven't seen the ghost for ages.

Clark: I think maybe we scared in off for good.

(*They exit the stage.*)

(*Ghost comes in and sits on a chair. He is crying. Virginia walks in.*)

Virginia: Why are you crying, Sir Simon? (*She puts her arm around his shoulder to comfort him.*)

Sir Simon: Because your brothers keep playing nasty tricks on me.

Virginia: They would stop if you behaved yourself.

Sir Simon: But I'm a ghost. I have to rattle my chains and moan and groan and walk around at night.

Virginia: You have been wicked. You murdered your wife. It's wrong to kill people.

Sir Simon: I know but her brother captured me and starved me to death.

Virginia: You poor ghost.

Sir Simon: Please help me. I'm so unhappy and so very tired.

Virginia: Have you not slept?

Sir Simon: I haven't slept for 500 years.

Virginia: I don't know how I can help.

Sir Simon: You could. Do you remember the note you found?

Virginia: (*Takes it out of her pocket and reads it.*) But I don't know what it means.

Sir Simon: It means that you must come with me to my chamber and pray for me.

Virginia: That sound easy enough.

Sir Simon: No person has ever entered the chamber and come out alive.

Virginia: I'll come with you.

(Off they go and disappear.)
(Mrs Otis and the other children come on stage looking for Virginia.)
Mrs Otis: Where is she?
Mr Otis: I'm getting worried.
(Then they hear a crash and she comes out of the secret chamber.)
Mrs Otis: Where have you been?
Virginia: I've been with the ghost. He knows he has been wicked and he is very sorry for everything. He gave me this box of jewels.
(They all look at the expensive jewels.)

Final scene: At the Graveyard

(There is a gravestone that's says "Sir Simon Canterville RIP." The whole family, Mrs. Umney and Lord Canterville all walk in and bow their heads in respect.)
Lord Canterville: Finally he is at peace.
Virginia: He is happy at last.

The Devoted Friend

Characters: Two villagers, Water Rat, Duck, Ducklings (as many as you want), green Linnet, Little Hans, Big Hugh, Big Hugh's wife, Big Hugh's son.

Villager 1: One morning the old water rat decided to leave his hole and go for a stroll.

Villager 2: While outside he came across a duck who was teaching her children to swim.

Duck: Now children, look at me very carefully I'm going to show you how to stand on your head.

(Ducklings are not listening to the duck, they are playing with one another having fun.

Water Rat: Duck, what naughty children you have.

Duck: They are not naughty. Everyone must start somewhere. When you are a parent you must be kind and patient.

Water Rat: Well, I've never been married and I've never had children. I think love is overrated and all one needed are friends for there is nothing in this world nobler or rarer than a devoted friend.

Green Linnet: Sorry to interrupt, water Rat, but I'm serious what is your idea of a devoted friend.

Duck: Good question, Green Linnet. Water Rat I'm very interested in your answer,

Water Rat: Green Linnet, what a silly question? Why a devoted friend should be devoted to me of course?

Green Linnet: What do you expect in return for this devotion.

Water Rat: I don't understand your question.

Green Linnet: Well, let me explain. I'll tell you a story.

Water Rat: Is the story about me?

Green Linnet: It applies to you so listen very carefully.... Once upon a time there was an honest man called little Hans. He lived in a cottage all by himself and everyday he worked in his garden

Little Hans: There is no garden in the land that is as lovely as mine, I've all types of flowers growing here such as sweet Williams, Gilly Flowers, Shepherd's purses, yellow roses and gold violets.

Green Linnet: Little Hans had lots of friends but he had only one devoted friend called big Hugh the miller.

Big Hugh: Hello Little Hans, I'm just passing and I thought I would help myself, to a large nosegay, some herbs and pocketful full of pines. Real friends should have everything in common.

Villager 1: Little Hans, don't you think it is very strange that Big Hugh, never gives you anything in return for your stuff.

Villager 2: He is rich. He has hundreds of sacks of flour, six cows as well as a flock of woolly sheep.

Little Hans: I'm don't worry about these matters. I enjoy the wonderful things that Big Hugh says about our friendship.

Green Linnet: Little Hans, worked his way in his garden during the spring, summer, Autumn but when winter came ….

Little Hans: I've no fruit or flowers to sell at the market I've no money and I'm cold and hungry. I'm off to bed without any supper.

Green Linnet: During Winter, Little Hans was very lonely because Big Hugh the miller never came to see him.

Big Hugh's Wife: My dear husband, why haven't you gone to see Little Hans.

Big Hugh: There is no point going to see Little Hans when he is starving. When people are in trouble they should be left alone and not be bothered by visitors. I shall wait till spring comes and then I'll pay him a visit because then he will give me a basket of flowers and fruit. That will make him so happy.

Big Hugh's Wife: You are very thoughtful and a devoted friend.

Big Hugh's Son: I've an idea why don't we ask Little Hans for dinner. He could have my supper.

Big Hugh: I don't know why I send you to school. You are so silly. If we invited Little Hans up here. He might get very envious if he saw our warm fire, wholesome food and cask of wine. He. Isn't even ask for some flour on credit and you know I couldn't do that.

Green Linnet: The son was very embarrassed and hung his head in shame that he had asked such a silly question.

Water Rat: Is that the end of the story?

Green Linnet: No, of course not. After winter passed, the miller said to his wife.

Miller: I'm going down to see Little Hans.

Big Hugh's Wife: What a good heart you have. Here take the basket and fill it up with beautiful flowers.

(Miller visits Little Hans with the basket in his hands.

Big Hugh: Good Morning, Little Hans.

Little Hans: Good morning.

Big Hugh: How have you been all winter?

Little Hans: How very kind of you to ask. I'm afraid I had a rather tough time but spring is here and I'm happy that all my flowers and herbs are doing well.

Big Hugh: How lovely your flowers look.

Little Hans: They are very lovely. I've to see them at the market and I'm going t to buy back my wheelbarrow.

Big Hugh: You sold your wheelbarrow what a silly thing to do.

Little Hans: Winter was very hard. I had no money so I sold it to buy some bread but I'm going to buy it back.

Big Hugh: I'll give you my wheelbarrow. One side is gone and it is in disrepair but despite that I'll give it to you. Now, I know it is very generous of me but you are my devoted friend.

Little Hans: It is generous of you. Thank you so much. I can fix it with that plank of wood over there.

Big Hugh: Why that plank of wood is just what I need to fix the hole in my roof, now, I've promised you the wheelbarrow you must give me that pal k of wood. Of course, the wheelbarrow is more expensive than the plank of weed but I'm a devoted friend and don't notice things like that. Here is my basket, please fill it with flowers and herbs.

Little Hans: It is a very big basket. I need the flowers to sell at the market tomorrow.

Big Hugh: I've given you my wheelbarrow and I don't think that is a lot to ask I. Exchange.

Little Hans: Of course, my dear friend you are welcome to all my flowers in the garden.

(Big Hugh leaves with a basket full of flowers and the plank of wood under his arm.))

Green Linnet: The next day, the miller came to Little Hans' house with a large bag of flour.

Big Hugh: Little Hans, can you take this bag of flour to market for me.

Little Hans: I'm busy today. I've to tend to my garden.

Big Hugh: Well, considering I'm giving you my wheelbarrow. It is unfriendly to refuse.

Little Hans: Of course, I'll take it.

Green Linnet: The next day, Big Hugh came for his money.

Big Hugh: Little Hans, come repair my roof with the plank of wood you gave me.

Little Hans: I need to work in my garden.

Big Hugh: Well, considering I'm giving you my wheelbarrow. It is unfriendly to refuse.

Little Hans: I'm sorry, of course I'll repair your roof.

Green Linnet: The next day.

Big Hugh: Little Hans, Come and drive my sheep to the mountain.

Little Hans: I need to work in my garden.

Big Hugh: Well, considering I'm giving you my wheelbarrow. It is unfriendly to refuse.

Little Hans: I'm sorry, of course I'll drive you sheep to the mountain.

Green Linnet: He was never able to tend to his garden as his devoted friend called everyday with tasks for him to do.

Little Hans: The flowers in my garden will think I've forgotten him. Big Hugh is my devoted friend and he is going to give me his wheelbarrow and that is a pure act of kindness.

Green Linnet: One night, while he was sitting by his fire, there was a loud knock at the door. It was Big Hugh.

Big Hugh: Dear Little Hans, I'm in trouble and need your help. My little boy has fallen off a ladder and hurt himself and he needs the doctor. But the doctor lives faraway. Could you fetch the doctor? You know I am giving you my wheelbarrow and so it is only fair that you do something for me in return.

Little Hans: Of course, I will help you. Can you lend me you lantern it is such a dark night I'm afraid I might fall into a ditch?

Big Hugh: I'm so sorry but the lantern is new, I couldn't bare to part with it.

Little Hans: Never mind, I will go without it.

Villager 1: Eventually Little Hans reached the doctor's house.

Doctor: Yes, what is it?

Little Hans: Big Hugh's son fell off a ladder you need to come immediately.

Doctor: All right. *(He grabs his bag, lantern and rides off on his horse.)*

Villager 2: The storm got worse. The rain was torrential and Little Hans couldn't see where he was going.

Villager 1: He wandered off on the moors and fell off the cliff to his death. Everyone turned up to his funeral as he was so popular.

Villager 2: Little Hans is a great loss to everyone.

Big Hugh: Well he is the biggest loss to me. I had nearly given him my wheelbarrow and now I don't know what to do about it. It is very much in my way at home and it is such bad repair I would get nothing for it if I sold it. One always suffers for being generous.

Water Rat: Well, what happened then?

Green Linnet: That's the end.

Water Rat: What became of Big Hugh?

Green Linnet: I don't know and I'm quite sure I don't care.

Water Rat: You have no sympathy in your nature.

Green Linnet: I'm afraid you don't quite see the moral.

Water Rat: Do you mean the story has a moral?

Green Linnet: Certainly.

Water Rat: *(angrily)* I think you should have told me that before you began. If you had done so I certainly would not have listened.

(Water Rat whisks his tail and goes back into his hole in a huff Mother duck comes up to the Green Linnet.)

Mother Duck: What's the matter with him?

Green Linnet: I'm afraid I've upset him. I told him a story with a moral.

Mother Duck: That is always a dangerous thing to do.

Green Linnet: I quite agree.

The Remarkable Rocket

Characters: Three narrators, King, Prince, Page, King's subjects (this number is flexible), reindeers (this number is flexible), Royal Pyrotechnist, Catherine Wheel, Bengal Light, Little Squib, Remarkable Rocket, Cracker, Fire Balloon, A workman, Frog, Duck, DragonFly, two boys, Goose.

Narrator 1: Once upon a time, the King's son was engaged to be married to a beautiful woman. He had waited a year for her to arrive.

(The king, prince, page, and king's subjects are moving around the stage. They look impatient and they keep looking at their watches.)

Narrator 2: She was a Russian princess and had to drive all the way from Russia in a sled drawn by reindeer.

(The princess enters the stage in her sled.)

Narrator 3: When the prince saw the beautiful princess, he dropped to his knees and kissed her hand.

Prince: Your photo was beautiful, but you are more beautiful in person.

Page: She was like a white rose before, but she is like a red rose now.

King's Subjects: White rose, red rose. White rose, red rose. White rose, red rose.

King: I'm so happy. Page, how much do I pay you?

Page: Nothing, your majesty. *(He bows.)*

King: Well, double it.

Page: *(looks at the audience.)* Double of nothing is nothing. *(Turns to the king and bows again.)* Thank you, your majesty. What an honour. It is quite clear that they love each other very much.

King: I will double your salary again.

Narrator 1: The celebrations continued for three days.

Narrator 2: Everybody ate, drank, and danced. *(Music plays in the background and everyone mimes eating and drinking, and dances to the music.)*

King: Quiet, everyone! Thank you very much for coming to celebrate the royal wedding. I hope you had a good time. We have one last surprise for the princess. There will be a grand display of fireworks at midnight.

Princess: I've never seen fireworks. What are they like?

Prince: They are like stars, but more beautiful. Everyone should rest before tonight's big event.

(Everyone exits stage left. The royal pyrotechnist and the fireworks enter stage right.)

Narrator 3: At the end of the king's garden, a great stand had been set up.

Royal Pyrotechnist: I must put the fireworks in place. You go here and you go there.

(He moves the fireworks around, one by one, until they are all lined up in a row.)

Little Squib: The world is certainly very beautiful. Just look at those yellow tulips. Why, if they were real crackers, they could not be lovelier. I am very glad I have travelled. Travel improves the mind wonderfully, and does away with all of one's prejudices.

Roman Candle: The King's garden is not the world, you foolish squib. The world is an enormous place, and it would take you three days to see it thoroughly.

Catherine Wheel: Any place you love is the world to you, but love is not fashionable anymore, the poets have killed it. They wrote so much about it that nobody believed them, and I am not surprised. True love suffers, and is silent. Romance is a thing of the past.

Roman Candle: Nonsense, romance never dies. It is like the moon, and lives forever. The bride and bridegroom, for instance, love each other very dearly. I heard all about them this morning from a brown-paper cartridge, who happened to be staying in the same drawer as myself and knew the latest Court news.

Catherine Wheel: *(shakes her head)* Romance is dead, romance is dead.

Remarkable Rocket: *(coughs)* How fortunate it is for the King's son, that he is to be married on the very day on which I am to be let off. Really, if it had been arranged beforehand, it could not have turned out better for him. But princes are always lucky.

Little Squib: Dear me! I thought it was quite the other way, and that we were to be let off in the Prince's honour.

Remarkable Rocket: I am a very remarkable Rocket, and come of remarkable parents. My mother was the most celebrated Catherine Wheel of her day, and was renowned for her graceful dancing. When she made her great public appearance, she spun around nineteen times before she went out, and each time that she did so, she threw into the air seven pink stars. She was three and a half feet in diameter, and made of the very best gunpowder. My father was a Rocket like myself, and of French extraction. He flew so high that the people were afraid that he would never come down again. He did, though, for he was of a kindly disposition, and he made a most brilliant descent in a shower of golden rain. The newspapers wrote about his performance in very flattering terms. Indeed, the Court Gazette called him a triumph of Pylotechnic art.

Bengal Light: Pyrotechnic, Pyrotechnic, you mean. I know it is Pyrotechnic, for I saw it written on my own canister.

Remarkable Rocket: *(annoyed)* Well, that's what I said. Pylotechnic. Now, what was I saying?

Roman Candle: You were talking about yourself.

Remarkable Rocket: Of course; I knew I was discussing some interesting subject when I was so rudely interrupted. I hate rudeness and bad manners of every kind, for I am extremely sensitive. No one in the whole world is as sensitive as I am, I am quite sure of that.

Cracker: What's a sensitive person?

Roman Candle: A person who, because he has corns himself, always treads on other people's toes.

Cracker: Ha, ha. Don't make me laugh too much, I'll explode.

Remarkable Rocket: *(angrily)* What are you laughing at, Cracker?

Cracker: I'm laughing because I'm happy.

Remarkable Rocket: What right have you to be happy? You should be thinking about others. In fact, you should be thinking about me. I am always thinking about myself, and I expect everybody else to do the same. That is what is called sympathy. It is a beautiful virtue, and I possess it to a high degree. Suppose, for instance, anything happened to me to-night. What a misfortune that would be for everyone! The Prince and Princess would never be happy again, their whole married life would be spoiled; and as for the King, I know he would not get over it. Really, when I begin to reflect on the importance of my position, I am almost moved to tears.

Roman Candle: If you want to give people pleasure, then you should keep yourself dry. (*He gives Remarkable Rocket a tissue but the Rocket refuses to take it.*)

Bengal Light: That's only common sense.

Remarkable Rocket: You forget that I am very uncommon, and very remarkable. Why, anybody can have common sense, provided that they have no imagination. But I have imagination, for I never think of things as they really are; I always think of them as being quite different. As for keeping myself dry, there is evidently no one here who can at all appreciate an emotional nature. Fortunately for myself, I don't care. The only thing that sustains one through life is the consciousness of the immense inferiority of everybody else, and this is a feeling that I have always cultivated. But none of you have any hearts. Here you are, laughing and making merry, just as if the Prince and Princess have not just been married.

Fire balloon: You had really better keep yourself dry. That is the important thing.

Remarkable Rocket: Very important for you, I have no doubt, but I shall weep if I choose.

Narrator 1: The Remarkable Rocket burst into real tears, which flowed down his stick like raindrops.

Catherine Wheel: He must have a true romantic nature, for he weeps when there is nothing at all to weep about.

Roman Candle: Oh, humbug.

Narrator 2: Then the moon rose like a wonderful silver shield; and the stars began to shine, and a sound of music came from the palace. The Prince and Princess were leading the dance.

Narrator 3: Then ten o'clock struck, and then eleven, and then twelve. And at the last stroke of midnight, everyone came out on the terrace, and the King sent for the Royal Pyrotechnist.

King: Let the fireworks begin.

Royal Pyrotechnist: Certainly, your majesty. (*He makes a low bow, and marches down to the end of the garden and sets the fireworks alight.*)

Prince: What a magnificent display!

Catherine Wheel: Whizz! Whizz! (*She spins around and around.*)

Roman Candle: Boom! Boom!

Little Squib. Time to party. (*He dances all over the stage.*)

Bengal Light: I've made everything look scarlet.

Fire Balloon: Good-bye, friends. (*He soars off into the sky.*)

Cracker: Bang! Bang!

Narrator 1: Everyone was a great success except the Remarkable Rocket. He was so damp from crying that he could not go off at all. The best thing in him was the gunpowder, and that was so wet with tears that it was of no use.

Narrator 2: All of his poor relations, to whom he would never speak, except with a sneer, shot up into the sky like wonderful, golden flowers with blossoms of fire.

Princess: Wow, this amazing! (*She laughs with pleasure.*)

Remarkable Rocket: I suppose they are reserving me for some grand occasion.

(*Everyone has left the stage except for the Remarkable Rocket. A workman enters.*)

Workman: There is a lot of cleaning up to do. What's this? It is a useless rocket. I'll just throw it away. (*Throws the Rocket over the wall.*)

Remarkable Rocket: Did he just call me a grand rocket? It's very uncomfortable here, but no doubt it is some fashionable watering-place, and they have sent me away to regain my health. My nerves are certainly very much shattered, and I require rest. (*Enter a frog.*)

Frog: (*looks at the Rocket with interest.*) A new arrival. Well, after all, there is nothing like mud. Give me rainy weather and a ditch, and I am quite happy. Do you think it will be a wet afternoon? I am sure that I hope so, but the sky is quite blue and cloudless. What a pity!

Remarkable Rocket: Ahem! Ahem!

Frog: What a delightful voice you have. Really, it is quite like a croak, and croaking is, of course, the most musical sound in the world. You will hear our glee-club this evening. We sit in the old duck-pond close by the farmer's house, and as soon as the moon rises, we begin. It is so entrancing that everybody lies awake to listen to us. In fact, it was only yesterday that I heard the farmer's wife say to her mother that she could not get a wink of sleep at night on account of us. It is most gratifying to find oneself so popular.

Remarkable Rocket: Ahem! Ahem!

Frog: Well, good-bye. I have enjoyed our conversation very much, I assure you. (*Frog exits, but the Rocket doesn't see him leave. There is a dragonfly sitting on a leaf.*)

Remarkable Rocket: You have talked the whole time about yourself. That is not conversation. You are a very irritating person and very ill-bred. I hate people who talk about themselves, as you do, when one wants to talk about oneself, as I do. It is what I call selfishness, and selfishness is a most detestable thing, especially to anyone of my temperament, for I am well-known for my sympathetic nature. In fact, you should take example by me. You could not possibly have a better model. Now that you have the chance, you had better avail yourself of it, for I am going back to Court almost immediately. I am a great favourite at Court; in fact, the Prince and Princess were married yesterday in my honour. Of course, you know nothing of these matters, for you are a provincial.

DragonFly: There is no good talking to him, no good at all, for he has gone away.

Remarkable Rocket: Well, that is his loss, not mine. I am not going to stop talking to him merely because he pays no attention. I like hearing myself talk. It is one of my greatest pleasures. I often have long conversations all by myself, and I am so clever that sometimes I don't understand a single word of what I am saying.

Dragon Fly: I can't listen to this. I'm off.

Remarkable Rocket: How very silly of him not to stay here. I am sure that he has not often got such a chance of improving his mind. However, I don't care a bit. Genius like mine is sure to be appreciated someday. (*Duck enters the stage.*)

Duck: Quack, quack. What a curious shape you are! May I ask, were you born like that, or is it the result of an accident?

Remarkable Rocket: It is quite evident that you have always lived in the country, otherwise you would know who I am. However, I excuse your ignorance. It would be unfair to expect other people to be as remarkable as myself. You will no doubt be surprised to hear that I can fly up into the sky, and come down in a shower of golden rain.

Duck: Well, I don't think much of that, as I cannot see what use it is to anyone. Now, if you could plough the fields like the ox, or draw a cart like the horse, or look after the sheep like the collie-dog, now that would be something.

Remarkable Rocket: My good creature, I see that you belong to the lower orders. A person of my position is never useful. We have certain accomplishments, and that is more than sufficient. I have no sympathy myself with industry of any kind, least of all with such industries as you seem to recommend. Indeed, I have always been of the opinion that hard work is simply the refuge of people who have nothing whatsoever to do.

Duck: Well, well, everybody has different tastes. I hope, at any rate, that you are going to take up your residence here.

Remarkable Rocket: I am merely a visitor, a distinguished visitor. The fact is that I find this place rather tedious. There is neither society here, nor solitude. In fact, it is essentially suburban. I shall probably go back to Court, for I know that I am destined to make a sensation in the world.

Duck: I'm bored and I'm hungry. It's time to leave.

Remarkable Rocket: Come back! Come back. I've a great deal to say to you. I am glad that she has gone, for she had a decidedly middle-class mind.

Narrator 1: The rocket began to think about the loneliness of genius, when suddenly two little boys came running down the bank, with a kettle and some faggots.

Boy 1: Look at that old stick.

Remarkable Rocket: He said gold stick.

Boy 2: We could use it in the fire.

Narrator 2: So they piled the faggots together, and put the Rocket on top, and lit the fire and fell asleep.

Remarkable Rocket: Now I am going off. I know I shall go much higher than the stars, much higher than the moon, much higher than the sun. In fact, I shall go so high that—

Narrator 3: Fizz! Fizz! Fizz! And he went straight up into the air.

Remarkable Rocket: Delightful! I shall go on like this forever. What a success! Now I am going to explode. I shall set the whole world on fire, and make such a noise that nobody will talk about anything else for a whole year.

Narrator 1: He certainly did explode. Bang! Bang! Bang! went the gunpowder. There was no doubt about it.

Narrator 2: But nobody heard him, not even the two little boys, for they were sound asleep.

Narrator 3: Then, all that was left of him was the stick, and this fell down on the back of a goose who was taking a walk by the side of the ditch.

Goose: Good heavens! It is raining sticks; I better rush back into the pond where I will be safe. (*Goose rushes into the pond.*)

Remarkable Rocket: I knew I would create a great sensation. (*He gasps and is extinguished.*)

The Nightingale and the Rose

Characters: Narrator, Young Student, Professor's Daughter, Nightingale, Green Lizard, Butterfly, White Rose Tree, Yellow Rose Tree, Red Rose Tree.

(Curtains open. The scene is a garden and a nightingale is perched on a tree, and a young man is in the centre of the stage. He looks very upset.)

Young Student: I'm in love with the professor's daughter. She said she would dance with me if I brought her red roses, but I've looked and looked and I couldn't find one red rose in my garden.

Nightingale: At last, I finally found a true lover.

Young Student: *(crying)* The Prince is giving a ball tomorrow tonight and my love, the professor's daughter, will be there. If I bring her a red rose, she will dance with me till dawn. If I bring her a red rose, I shall hold her in my arms, we will hold hands and gaze lovingly into each other's eyes all night. Sadly, there is no red rose in my garden, so I shall sit alone, and she will ignore me, and my heart will break. *(The young student is on his knees crying. The nightingale looks on with sympathy. Enter the green lizard and the butterfly.)*

Green lizard: Nightingale, Why is the young student crying?'

Butterfly: Why indeed?

Nightingale: He is weeping for a red rose.

Green lizard and Butterfly: For a red rose? How very ridiculous.

(The butterfly flies off and the green lizard scuttles away. The nightingale starts to fly around the garden looking for a rose; he finds a rose tree.)

Nightingale: Rose tree, please give me a red rose.

White Rose Tree: My roses are white, as white as the foam of the sea, and whiter than the snow upon the mountain. But go to my brother who grows round the old sundial, and perhaps he will give you what you want.

Nightingale: Thank you. *(The nightingale flies off and goes round the sundial to the rose tree's brother.)*

Nightingale: Rose tree, please give me a red rose.

Yellow Rose Tree: My roses are yellow, as yellow as the hair of the mermaid who sits upon an amber throne, and yellower than the daffodil that blooms in the meadow before its mowed. But go to my brother who grows beneath the student's window, and perhaps he will give you what you want. (*The nightingale flies off and goes to the student's window to the rose tree's brother.*)

Nightingale: Rose tree, please give me a red rose.

Red Rose Tree: My roses are red, as red as the feet of the dove, and redder than the great fans of coral that wave in the ocean-cavern. But the winter has chilled my veins, and the frost has nipped my buds, and the storm has broken my branches, and I shall have no roses at all this year.

Nightingale: But I only want one red rose.

Red Rose Tree: If you want a red rose, you must build it out of music by moonlight, and stain it with your own heart's blood. You must sing to me with your breast against a thorn. All night long you must sing to me, and the thorn must pierce your heart, and your life-blood must flow into my veins, and become mine.

Nightingale: Death is a great price to pay for a red rose. Yet love is better than life, and what is the heart of a bird compared to the heart of a man?'

Narrator: That night, the moon shone in the heavens. The nightingale flew to the rose tree and set her breast against the thorn. All night long she sang with her breast against the thorn, and the cold crystal moon leaned down and listened. All night long she sang, and the thorn went deeper and deeper into her breast, and her life-blood ebbed away from her.

Red Rose Tree: Press closer, little nightingale, or the day will come before the rose is finished.

Nightingale: The rose has turned into the most beautiful red colour. It's as red as a ruby.

Narrator: As day came, the nightingale's voice grew fainter, and her little wings began to beat, and her eyes began to slowly close. Fainter and fainter grew her song, and she felt something choking her in her throat.

Red Rose Tree: Look, look, the rose is finished now. (*The nightingale looks at the rose and dies with a smile on her face. The young student looks out his window and see the red rose. He is delighted and starts to jump up and down.*)

Young Student: What a wonderful piece of luck. Here is a red rose! I have never seen any rose like it in all my life. It is so beautiful. (*He leans down and plucks it. Then he puts on his hat and runs*

34

up to the professor's house with the rose in his hand. The professor's daughter greets him.)

Young Student: You said that you would dance with me if I brought you a red rose. Here is the reddest rose in all the world. You will wear it tonight next your heart, and as we dance together, it will tell you how I love you.'

Professor's Daughter: I am afraid it will not go with my dress, and, besides, the chamberlain's nephew has sent me some real jewels, and everybody knows that jewels cost far more than flowers.

Young Student: *(angrily)* You are very ungrateful. (*He throws the rose into the street, where it falls into the gutter.)*

Professor's Daughter: Ungrateful! I tell you what, you are very rude, and, after all, who are you? Only a student. Why, I don't believe you have even got silver buckles to your shoes as the chamberlain's nephew has. (*She storms off and slams the door in his face.).*

Young Student: What a silly thing love is. It is not half as useful as logic, for it does not prove anything, and it is always telling one of things that are not going to happen, and making one believe things that are not true. In fact, it is quite unpractical, and, as in this age, to be practical is everything. I shall go back to philosophy and study metaphysics.

Narrator: So, he returned to his room and pulled out a great dusty book and began to read.

(Student goes back to his room and takes out the book and blows off the dust.) Curtains close.

Other Books by the Author:

Drama Start Series:
Drama Start: Drama Activities, Plays and Monologues for Children (Ages 3-8)
Drama Start Two: Drama Activities for Children (Ages 9-12)
Stage Start: 20 Plays for Children (Ages 3-12)
Stage Start: 20 More Plays for Children (Ages 3-12)
Movement Start: Over 100 Movement Activities and Stories for Children
ESL Drama Start: Drama Activities and Plays for ESL Learners

On Stage Series:
Fairy Tales on Stage: A Collection of Plays for Children
Classics on Stage: A Collection of Plays Based on Classic Children's Stories
Aesop's Fables on Stage: A Collection of Plays Based on Aesop's Fables
Christmas Stories on Stage: A Collection of Plays for Children
Panchatantra on Stage: A Collection of Plays for Children
Hans Christian Andersen's Stories on Stage: A Collection of Plays for Children

If you enjoyed this book, I would appreciate it if you would leave a review. Please click here.

Printed in Great Britain
by Amazon